Instagram Sponsorships & UGC Deals

Charge More, Negotiate Better & Land Big Brands

By Joe Correa

Published by Live Stronger Faster

This book is for educational and informational purposes only. The author and publisher are not engaged in rendering legal, financial, or other professional advice. Readers should consult a qualified professional before making any financial decisions.

First Edition

Table of Contents

Introduction

In the evolving landscape of social media in 2025, Instagram has become one of the most powerful platforms for creators who want to turn their creativity into income, and nowhere is this more evident than in the world of brand deals, sponsorships, and UGC (User-Generated Content). While millions of users scroll through Reels, Stories, and carousel posts every day, only a small percentage realize that these same posts can become consistent, predictable revenue streams through paid collaborations with companies eager to reach new audiences. Yet despite this massive opportunity, most aspiring influencers and UGC creators have no idea how to land paid deals, how to pitch themselves effectively, or how to confidently negotiate higher rates—often leaving thousands of dollars on the table. This book exists to change that by giving you the exact systems, scripts, frameworks, and psychology you need to transform your Instagram presence into a professional brand-partner magnet, even if you have a small following, a faceless page, or are just starting out.

What most creators don't realize is that brands today care far less about follower counts and far more about content quality, niche alignment, storytelling skills, and conversion potential. Thanks to the explosion of UGC creators and micro-influencers, companies now understand that one polished video from a skilled creator can outperform a massive influencer with millions of followers. This shift has empowered everyday people to monetize their creativity without being internet-famous, without showing their face if they prefer anonymity, and without spending years trying to "build an audience" before making money. In fact, one of the fastest-growing creator categories is the UGC creator who doesn't rely on followers at all—they get paid purely for producing videos, photos, and Reels that brands use for ads. This book will show you how to position yourself as a valuable content partner, stand out in a crowded creator market, and build a brand-deal business that pays you over and over again for the same skill set you're already using on Instagram every day.

However, success in Instagram brand deals requires more than good content. It demands a deep understanding of brand psychology, pricing strategies, negotiation tactics, and outreach systems that run even while you sleep. One of the biggest mistakes creators make is underpricing themselves because they don't know industry standards or how much brands really spend on influencer marketing. In 2025, brands are pouring record amounts into Instagram campaigns because the platform drives better engagement, deeper trust, and more purchase intent than almost any other social network. That means even creators with 2,000 followers can earn hundreds per post, and emerging creators with 20,000 followers can make more from sponsorships than many full-time jobs. Once you understand how to calculate your value—based on niche, content type, engagement, usage rights, and deliverables—you unlock the ability to confidently charge premium rates and negotiate deals that pay you what you're worth. Throughout this introduction and entire book, you'll learn the real numbers, including rate formulas, negotiation templates, and pricing tiers brands won't tell you about.

Another pillar of high-earning creators is the ability to create systems that attract deals automatically. Most creators rely on luck: hoping a brand notices them or waiting for random inquiries to show up in their DMs. Top creators take the opposite approach. They proactively build automated outreach pipelines, use AI tools to write persuasive pitches, create media kits that instantly establish authority, and implement follow-up systems that convert "no response" into "paid partnership." The truth is that creators who treat brand deals like a business land far more sponsorships than those who treat it like a hobby. In this book, you'll learn how to use AI content generators, CRM tools, automation platforms, email sequences, pitch templates, and negotiation scripts to build a professional brand-deal machine that gets you collaborations consistently, not occasionally. You'll also learn the psychology behind outreach—what brands look for, how to position yourself as a solution to their marketing problems, and how to frame your content as a revenue-producing asset rather than just a pretty video.

Even more important is knowing how to negotiate like a professional. Many creators fear negotiation because they don't want to "lose the deal," but this fear leads to chronic undercharging and burnout. The truth is that brands expect negotiation. They build negotiation room into their budgets. They respect creators who know their value. And they prefer working with confident creators who operate with clarity, professionalism, and structure. In this book, you'll learn exactly what to say when a brand lowballs you, how to counter professionally, how to request usage rights fees, how to price whitelisting permissions, and how to secure long-term partnerships. You'll learn how to turn a single $300 deal into a $3,000 monthly retainer, how to anchor your pricing so brands perceive higher value, and how to negotiate without pressure or emotion using psychology-based scripts that feel natural and ethical. You'll also discover how to protect yourself legally by understanding contracts, deliverables, deadlines, revisions, and intellectual property—all in simple creator-friendly language.

One of the strongest advantages of brand deals and UGC is their ability to create high-income opportunities for creators in any niche. Whether you produce beauty tutorials, fitness content, real estate tips, finance insights, tech reviews, lifestyle videos, parenting content, food recipes, gaming clips, or faceless POV Reels, there are brands looking for creators exactly like you. In fact, many of the most lucrative niches are not the ones people assume—they're niches like productivity, home improvement, wellness, personal finance, skincare, pets, and health tech, where brands have deep marketing budgets and long-term ad cycles. This book will show you how to identify the most profitable niches, how to align your content with high-budget brands, and how to reverse-engineer what top creators are doing so you can replicate their success in your own niche—even if you feel like your content isn't "special" yet. You'll also learn how to build an irresistible creator identity and message that attracts brands who want to work with you before you even pitch them.

Finally, this book is designed to help you build a long-term, sustainable brand-deal business. The goal isn't simply to get a few one-off sponsorships. The real goal is to create a system where brands return to you month after month, where your content becomes an asset that keeps paying you, and where your influence grows in a way that generates additional opportunities such as affiliate income, digital product sales, Reels bonuses, UGC packages, and multi-platform partnerships. You'll learn how to build authority through storytelling, how to optimize your Instagram profile to attract brand collaborations, how to showcase your portfolio even as a beginner, and how to transition from small deals to major partnerships with national and global brands. Whether you're a creator aiming to earn $1,000 per month or an ambitious entrepreneur wanting to build a $10,000–$20,000/month creator business, this book will guide you step-by-step with the exact strategies used by successful influencers and UGC creators.

Chapter 1

Understanding the Brand Deal Economy

The world of Instagram sponsorships and UGC deals is built on a simple truth: brands need creators more than creators need brands. Even the largest companies in the world can no longer succeed with traditional advertising alone, because consumers prefer real people, relatable stories, authentic product demonstrations, and native content that blends naturally into their daily feed. This shift has created a massive demand for creators who know how to communicate, storytell, and influence purchasing decisions through Instagram content. To understand how to succeed in brand deals, it's essential to understand the brand deal economy itself—the psychology, the budget flow, the decision-making process, and the reason companies choose certain creators over others. Most people wrongly believe that brands only work with creators who have massive followings. In reality, brands prioritize creators who can generate authentic content, maintain trust with their audience, and demonstrate a visual style that matches the brand's identity. Even UGC creators who have no followers at all can earn thousands per month simply by producing content that brands use for ads, emails, and product pages. The creator economy is expanding rapidly, and understanding its mechanics gives you a huge advantage when positioning yourself to land paid sponsorships.

Brands invest heavily in Instagram because it offers concentrated attention, high trust, and an emotional connection that traditional ads can't replicate. When someone sees an ad on TV or a banner on a website, they know it was created by the company. But when they see a tutorial from a real person, a testimonial from a relatable voice, or a lifestyle video from someone they follow, the trust level increases dramatically. This trust translates directly into sales and brand awareness, which is why companies allocate significant portions of their marketing budget specifically for influencer and UGC content. As a creator, you are stepping into a marketplace where brands are actively searching for partners who can tell stories, demonstrate products, and inspire buying decisions. Understanding that brands are constantly evaluating creators helps you see the bigger picture of why your content matters—not because it looks pretty but because it influences behavior. That influence is what brands pay for, and your job is to make it clear why your content is valuable.

Another key part of the brand deal economy is understanding how budgets work. Brands typically divide their marketing money into buckets: brand awareness, paid ads, influencer campaigns, UGC content, and evergreen creative assets. Many creators mistakenly assume that a brand's budget comes from a single pool. But in reality, even small companies may have multiple budgets dedicated specifically to creator partnerships. This means that "we don't have budget right now" rarely means they can't pay you; it often means you need to speak with a different department, send a better pitch, or position your content in a way that aligns with their goals. Large brands can spend tens of thousands per month on UGC alone and still look for new creators every week. Even mid-sized companies often run dozens of creator collaborations simultaneously. When you understand how budgets operate, it becomes easier to negotiate confidently, raise your rates, and secure ongoing partnerships instead of one-off deals. The brand deal economy rewards creators who understand the bigger picture, and this knowledge helps you stand out from those who simply send random pitches hoping for a response.

Another major factor in the creator economy is matching brand identity. Brands don't just look for creators—they look for alignment. They want creators whose aesthetic, values, tone, and lifestyle fit the narrative they want to project. This is why two creators with similar follower counts can receive drastically different brand deal opportunities. One might get paid consistently while the other receives mostly gifted offers. Brands choose creators who reflect the lifestyle they want their customers to feel. Whether your content is clean and minimalistic, high-energy and motivational, cozy and aesthetic, or bold and opinionated, your style is part of your brand identity. The clearer your identity, the faster brands understand what role you can play in their campaigns. Understanding this allows you to shape your Instagram presence intentionally—your bio, your highlights, your posting style, your captions, and even the color palette of your edits communicate who you are. Creators who understand this often attract deals without pitching because brands immediately know what they're getting. This alignment is one of the strongest forces driving paid sponsorships, making brand identity a crucial part of the brand deal economy.

Brands also evaluate content quality above all else. The rise of UGC creators proves that the number of followers does not determine your earnings; your ability to create high-quality, conversion-focused content does. Brands look for creators who understand lighting, camera angles, hooks, pacing, voiceovers, product placement, and storytelling. They pay for creators who know how to capture attention in the first few seconds of a Reel and maintain viewer interest long enough to make an impact. They value creators who can make a product feel natural instead of forced, and who know how to blend brand messaging with authentic storytelling. The creator economy is heavily driven by content performance, which means brands evaluate creators based on your content style rather than your audience size. This gives every creator a level playing field, allowing beginners to break into the market quickly by simply mastering content fundamentals and delivering consistent quality.

A crucial part of understanding the brand deal economy is recognizing how brands measure success. Brands evaluate content based on engagement, watch time, storytelling quality, brand fit, and conversion potential. Some brands care primarily about awareness; others track clicks, sales, sign-ups, or user-generated content that can be used across multiple marketing channels. UGC content, in particular, is often used for paid advertising rather than organic posting, meaning your content could be seen millions of times even if you have a small following. The better your content performs, the more likely brands are to hire you repeatedly. Brands also evaluate creators based on professionalism, communication speed, deadline reliability, and overall experience. These “soft skills” matter just as much as your content. Many creators lose opportunities not because of lack of talent but because they respond slowly, submit late deliverables, or communicate unprofessionally. Understanding how brands evaluate creators helps you stand out not just creatively but professionally, which is critical for securing long-term partnerships.

Finally, the brand deal economy rewards creators who treat their work like a business. The creators earning the highest incomes build systems for pitching, negotiating, tracking invoices, managing contracts, and delivering assets consistently. They understand industry rates, usage rights, licensing fees, and pricing structures. They invest in improving their skills, refining their brand identity, upgrading their equipment, and streamlining their workflow. They approach sponsorships strategically, aligning themselves with brands that support their content direction, audience lifestyle, and long-term growth. When you understand how the creator economy works, you stop seeing brand deals as random opportunities and start seeing them as predictable income streams you can build, scale, and automate. This chapter lays the foundation for everything that follows, helping you think like a creator who earns consistently by understanding the business side of Instagram sponsorships and UGC deals.

"The Deal That Opened Her Eyes"

When Elena first started posting beauty tutorials on Instagram, she never imagined her content could earn her money. She simply enjoyed sharing her morning routines, product favorites, and simple makeup tips with her small but supportive audience. Her following grew slowly, but she never thought of herself as an influencer. She watched bigger creators land sponsorships and assumed that world was reserved for the glamorous, the famous, or the ones with cameras she could never afford. Her content was filmed on her phone, lit by the sunlight from her apartment window, and edited with simple tools. She had passion but no real expectations. Until one day, a skincare brand messaged her asking if she would be interested in creating a tutorial featuring their new moisturizer. They offered her free product and exposure. Elena felt excited, flattered, and validated, but she also felt something else—confused. She didn't know how to respond or if she should ask for payment. She accepted the gifted collaboration, feeling grateful for the opportunity, unaware that this moment would open her eyes to a world she never knew she was already part of.

After she posted the video, something unexpected happened. The brand reached out again, saying her content performed better than they anticipated. They shared that her Reel brought in more website clicks than a campaign they had paid a larger influencer to run. They asked if she would be open to creating more content—this time as paid UGC. When Elena heard the term, she had no idea what it meant. The brand explained that they wanted her to create videos not for her page but for their advertisements. They didn't care about her follower count; they cared about the way she explained the product, the warmth in her storytelling, and how natural she appeared on camera. They saw value in her creativity that she had never seen in herself. They offered to pay her $300 for a single video—a number that shocked her because she had never earned money for her Instagram content before. She accepted with nervous excitement, unsure whether she deserved the payment, but eager to learn what this industry was about.

The more she worked with the brand, the more curious she became about the business behind sponsorships. She began researching how companies selected creators, how they measured performance, and why content like hers mattered so much to their marketing strategy. She learned that brands were shifting away from traditional ads because audiences didn't trust them anymore. People wanted authenticity, real experiences, and relatable demonstrations. She learned that even creators with small followings could earn significant income if they produced compelling content that aligned with brand messaging. She realized that the brand hadn't selected her because of her audience size—it selected her because she connected with viewers in a genuine, soothing way that made them feel understood. Her storytelling was her superpower, and she didn't even know she had one.

As she continued creating content, she noticed that other brands started liking her posts, saving her videos, and even resharing her tutorials. She began receiving DMs from companies offering gifted collaborations, but now she had a different mindset. Instead of feeling flattered, she started evaluating whether the collaboration aligned with her goals. She learned to ask about budget, usage rights, and timelines. She started recognizing that brands had structured marketing budgets specifically allocated for creators like her. It shocked her to learn that even small brands could spend thousands on UGC content every month. For the first time, she saw Instagram as more than a hobby—it could be a business. She felt empowered, excited, and determined to step into this new world with intention. She built a simple portfolio, refined her content style, and began pitching herself to brands she genuinely loved.

Her turning point came when a wellness brand she admired responded to her pitch. They said they had already seen her content online and had been waiting for the right campaign to reach out. They offered her a paid collaboration that included two Reels, one carousel, and one Story set. The rate they proposed was double what she would have asked for, and she realized she had been undervaluing herself all along. For the first time, she felt like a professional creator, not just someone posting for fun. She understood now that brands invested in creators because creators held the trust and attention that companies wanted. She realized she wasn't just making videos—she was shaping consumer decisions. Her content had impact, value, and meaning.

Over time, Elena refined her negotiation skills, upgraded her equipment, and improved her editing. She began securing ongoing partnerships with brands she loved, turning one-off deals into long-term collaborations. She discovered that companies valued reliability, clear communication, and professional delivery as much as creative talent. She became the creator brands relied on, recommended, and returned to month after month. She transformed from an unsure beginner to a confident, high-earning creator who understood the psychology and economics of brand deals. Yet she never forgot the collaboration that opened her eyes—the one that made her realize that brands were not doing her a favor by offering opportunities. She had been valuable all along; she simply needed to learn how to position herself, recognize her worth, and step boldly into the creator economy waiting for her.

Chapter 2

How Brands Evaluate Creators

To succeed in Instagram sponsorships and UGC deals, you must understand exactly how brands evaluate creators. Most new creators mistakenly believe that brands only care about follower counts, but that is one of the least important factors in the modern creator economy. Brands today care about influence, not numbers; impact, not vanity metrics; and storytelling, not perfection. Their decisions are based on criteria that most creators never think about, but once you understand these criteria, you can intentionally position yourself to win deals even if you have a small following or are just beginning. Brands evaluate creators through a multi-layered lens that includes content quality, brand alignment, storytelling approach, on-camera presence, relatability, niche expertise, engagement authenticity, and the creator's professionalism. When you understand the psychology behind each of these factors, you transform from a hopeful beginner into a strategic, high-value creator who knows exactly how to attract paid collaborations.

Content quality is one of the first things brands analyze. They look at how well you use lighting, sound, framing, pacing, editing, storytelling, hooks, and transitions. They want content that feels native to the platform while maintaining enough polish to reflect their brand standards. They examine your consistency to determine whether you can reliably produce quality content for them. Even if your Reels aren't viral, brands notice creators who have a strong visual identity, a confident speaking style, or a unique creative angle. They don't need you to be perfect—they need you to be intentional. Brands look for creators whose content naturally grabs attention within the first two seconds, maintains interest, provides clarity, and evokes a feeling. They want content that will make viewers think, "I want to try that" or "This looks like something I would use." When you understand this, you realize that improving your content quality is one of the fastest ways to increase your value and land more deals.

Another major factor is brand alignment. Brands want creators who look like their audience, think like their customers, and live within the lifestyle their marketing represents. If your content style matches their aesthetic—whether clean, bold, cozy, colorful, luxury, minimalistic, or earthy—you instantly rise to the top of their list. Brands also evaluate whether your values match theirs. A sustainable skincare brand, for example, wants creators who naturally talk about wellness and eco-friendly living. A fitness brand wants creators who are active and energetic. A tech brand wants creators who review gadgets with clarity and enthusiasm. The more aligned you appear with a brand's mission, audience, and visual identity, the more likely they are to hire you, even if your following is small. Many creators overlook this point and try to pitch every brand they see, but successful creators pitch strategically, understanding that brand alignment multiplies their chances of landing deals.

Engagement authenticity also plays a significant role in brand evaluations. Brands don't just look at likes and comments—they analyze the depth of your interactions. They want to see whether your audience reacts meaningfully to your content. If your comments include real conversations, product questions, personal messages, or emotional responses, it signals trust. Brands rely heavily on this trust because it predicts whether your sponsored content will perform well. They also analyze whether your engagement looks organic. Suspicious spikes, irrelevant comments, or inconsistent engagement ratios indicate that a creator may be artificially boosting their metrics. Brands today use software to analyze creator authenticity, so honest, natural engagement is far more valuable than inflated numbers. When you understand this, you stop focusing on follower count and start focusing on building a real connection with your community—even if it's small.

Another factor brands evaluate is your niche. Brands want to work with creators whose content matches their industry because it allows for more authentic integrations. Even if your niche is small, it can be more profitable than a large but unfocused page. For example, a skincare creator will receive more skincare brand deals than a lifestyle creator who occasionally posts about beauty. A finance creator will attract banks, budgeting apps, and fintech tools. A pet creator will attract dog brands, pet food companies, and pet tech. Brands love niche creators because their audiences are more targeted and more likely to convert. This means that clarifying your niche isn't just good for growth—it's essential for monetization. When your content demonstrates consistent expertise, storytelling, and interest within a niche, brands view you as a high-quality creator worth partnering with.

Professionalism might be one of the most overlooked but powerful factors in brand evaluations. Brands often choose creators who communicate clearly, follow instructions, meet deadlines, and maintain a positive attitude during collaboration. Many creators lose opportunities simply because they take too long to respond, submit low-effort work, or seem unorganized. Brands value creators who make their job easier, not harder. This includes understanding deliverables, asking the right questions, providing drafts when needed, and maintaining transparency. Creators who behave like professionals stand out because brands often deal with inconsistent or unreliable influencers. When you present yourself as someone who takes the partnership seriously, brands see you as a long-term asset, not just a one-off collaborator.

Brands also evaluate your ability to tell stories that sell without feeling like an ad. They analyze the first three seconds of your videos, your hook clarity, your pacing, your transitions, your voiceovers, your ability to showcase a product naturally, and your closing message. They want content that captures attention, demonstrates value, and inspires action. This isn't about being a salesperson; it's about being a storyteller. Brands pay for your ability to translate their product into a narrative that fits into the everyday life of your audience. When you master storytelling, you become more than a creator—you become a marketer. And that's when your rates increase dramatically.

Finally, brands analyze your potential for long-term collaboration. They look at whether your content direction aligns with their long-term marketing plans. They assess whether your style is evolving, whether your page is growing, and whether your community is becoming more engaged. Brands love creators who show momentum because momentum signals future influence. Long-term deals are far more valuable than one-off posts, and they often come with significantly higher pay. When you understand how brands evaluate creators, you gain clarity, control, and confidence. You stop wondering whether you are "good enough" and start optimizing your profile, content, and messaging to meet the criteria brands use every day. Once you understand their perspective, you unlock the ability to position yourself not just as a content creator but as a strategic partner that brands genuinely want to invest in.

"Why They Chose Maya"

Maya had always wondered how companies chose which creators to work with. She assumed it was all about follower counts and popularity, so she never considered herself a candidate for sponsorships. With only six thousand followers, she believed she wasn't "big" enough for brands to notice her. She posted fashion and wellness content consistently, but she didn't think her page stood out. That changed the day she received an email from a major activewear company asking if she would be interested in a paid partnership for their new leggings line. She reread the email four times, convinced it had to be a mistake. She wasn't a fitness influencer—not in the traditional sense—and she didn't understand why such a well-known brand would choose someone like her. But instead of responding with disbelief, she decided to ask the brand a simple question: what made them choose her? Their answer opened her eyes to the truth behind how brands evaluate creators, and it reshaped her understanding of her own value.

The brand's marketing manager explained that they had been watching Maya's content for months. They were drawn to her soft, warm aesthetic and her calming storytelling style. They loved the way she blended fashion with real-life moments—morning yoga, coffee rituals, walks with her dog, weekend resets. Her content didn't feel staged; it felt like a slice of life. They noticed her audience consistently left thoughtful comments asking where she bought her outfits, what size she wore, and what materials she preferred. Her engagement wasn't just high—it was meaningful. The brand told her they valued authenticity over audience size, and they believed her followers genuinely trusted her recommendations. For them, that trust was worth far more than a massive following. Hearing this shocked Maya because she had never considered engagement quality or brand alignment as factors brands cared about.

As Maya prepared for the partnership, she began seeing her content through the brand's eyes. She noticed how consistent her aesthetic was, how her lighting was always natural, how she framed her shots carefully even when she didn't realize it. She began to understand why her page appealed to the brand: her content aligned perfectly with the lifestyle their marketing team wanted to promote. They didn't need her to be a fitness influencer—they needed her to embody the feeling their customers desired. She realized that her style, her tone, her softness, and her relatability were all part of her unique creative identity. This realization made her approach the collaboration with newfound confidence. She didn't need to pretend to be someone else. She simply needed to amplify what she already did naturally.

After she posted the sponsored content, the brand reached out again—this time with analytics. Her Reel not only performed well on her page but also outperformed several creators with larger followings. Her video received more saves, more shares, and more comments from people expressing genuine interest. The brand told her that her authenticity was "rare" and that her audience behavior indicated strong trust. They introduced her to their paid UGC program and offered to hire her for additional videos strictly for their ads. They explained that they chose creators based on content quality, alignment, and reliability—not follower count. Maya felt a wave of clarity wash over her. She had been evaluating herself based on numbers, but brands had been evaluating her based on connection.

As she continued working with the brand, she began receiving messages from other companies—skincare brands, supplement companies, local boutiques, and even a travel agency. She realized that brands were paying attention to her consistency, her tone, and her professionalism. Every email she responded to quickly, every deliverable she submitted early, every collaboration she handled with care strengthened her reputation. She understood now that brands valued creators who made their job easier, who communicated well, and who delivered content that felt authentic. She realized that she had spent years underestimating her worth because she didn't understand how brands made decisions.

Eventually, one of the brands offered her a three-month contract—a long-term partnership that provided stability and increased earnings. They said the reason they chose her for the ongoing deal was her reliability and her ability to create content that consistently performed well. This moment shifted everything for Maya. She began seeing herself not just as a creator but as a professional partner in a growing industry. She understood that she wasn't selected by luck; she was selected because she embodied the qualities brands actively searched for.

The more she grew, the more she shared her journey with other small creators who felt unseen. She told them the truth she had learned firsthand: brands choose creators based on storytelling, relatability, alignment, consistency, and professionalism. She explained that follower count was never the deciding factor. Her journey became a reminder that creators who understand how brands evaluate them gain the power to position themselves intentionally and unlock opportunities they never thought were possible. And every time she landed a new collaboration, she remembered the moment she asked the simple question that changed everything: "Why did you choose me?" The answer revealed the reality of the creator economy—and it changed her life forever.

Chapter 3

Building a High-Value Creator Identity

Your creator identity is the foundation of your brand-deal success. It determines how brands perceive you, how they evaluate your strategic fit, and how confidently they decide to pay you. Most creators overlook their identity entirely, thinking that posting content is enough, but brands choose creators who present themselves as polished, intentional, and aligned with the company's message. Your creator identity is not just your niche—it includes your tone, visuals, personality, values, lifestyle, editing style, on-camera presence, storytelling approach, and overall energy. When brands look at your profile, they process it the way a hiring manager reviews a résumé, portfolio, and personality fit all at once. A strong creator identity communicates who you are in seconds and makes brands feel certain that you are the right fit for their campaigns. A weak creator identity forces brands to guess, and whenever brands must guess, they move on to someone else. Building a high-value identity is one of the most profitable investments you can make.

The creator identity begins with clarity. Brands want creators who know who they are and who they serve. If your content is all over the place, with no consistent message, aesthetic, or theme, brands struggle to understand how you would represent their product. But when your profile communicates a clear lifestyle or niche—beauty, wellness, tech, skincare, fashion, fitness, home improvement, food, finance, travel, or luxury—your identity becomes instantly recognizable. Brands want creators who embody a lifestyle, not creators who simply post content. Your identity should tell a story: the wellness creator who feels calm and grounding, the fashion creator who inspires confidence, the fitness creator who motivates action, the skincare creator who embodies glow and self-care. Once you understand the story your brand communicates, you can intentionally shape everything you post to reinforce that feeling. This clarity elevates your perceived value.

A strong creator identity also involves consistency. Brands analyze your feed to see whether your content maintains a coherent visual rhythm. They look for consistent lighting, editing, pacing, color palette, and tone. Consistency communicates professionalism because it shows you have a defined creative style. When a brand hires you, they are not just paying for a single video—they are paying for the predictability of your style. They want to know what their sponsored content will look like before you create it. If your profile is visually cohesive, brands feel safer investing in you. If your content swings wildly in style, vibe, or quality, brands feel uncertain. Consistency builds trust, and trust increases your rates. You don't need perfection; you need recognizable style.

Another part of your identity is your emotional tone. Every creator has an energy, whether they realize it or not. Some creators feel warm and friendly, others feel educational and precise, others feel bold and high-energy, while some feel calm and thoughtful. Brands pay close attention to tone because tone determines the emotional impact of your content. A wellness brand might choose a soft-spoken creator whose videos feel peaceful. A tech brand might choose a creator who speaks clearly with a confident pace. A fitness brand might choose someone energetic and motivating. Your tone becomes part of your identity, and the key is to lean into it rather than dilute it. When you embrace your natural communication style, you attract brands that align with your energy. When brands see emotional consistency, they classify you as a "fit" for certain campaigns, making you more likely to be chosen.

Professionalism is another element of your identity, and brands evaluate it before ever contacting you. They analyze your bio to see if it's clear, they look at your highlights to understand your content categories, they check whether your email is easy to find, and they pay attention to whether your page feels intentional or chaotic. A clean bio that communicates your niche and your value instantly elevates your identity. Highlights that are organized, labeled, and visually consistent show that you understand content curation. An email address or link in your bio communicates that you are open for business. These small details influence brand decisions far more than creators realize. A creator might have great content but lose deals because their profile feels unorganized or incomplete. Building a professional creator identity makes brands take you seriously before you ever pitch yourself.

Your creator identity also includes your message. This is the deeper purpose behind your content. Brands love creators who have a mission or clear narrative because it gives them confidence that you know who you are. For example, your message might be helping people feel confident in their skin, simplifying fitness for beginners, making fashion accessible, sharing honest product reviews, inspiring self-care routines, or promoting wellness from home. A clear message drives consistency, and consistency builds value. Brands trust creators who stand for something because it aligns with brand storytelling. When you define your message, your content becomes more powerful, relatable, and valuable to brands who want to join that story.

The final part of building a high-value identity is improvement. Brands love creators who show growth. They look for creators who refine their lighting, improve their editing, upgrade their equipment, and evolve their style. Growth signals long-term potential, and brands want creators who will become even more valuable over time. When your identity shows progression, brands see you not just as a creator but as a rising asset. Investing in your skills—storytelling, editing, on-camera confidence—translates directly into higher rates and better deals. Building a high-value creator identity is a strategic process, and once you understand how brands interpret your profile, you gain the power to shape that interpretation to your advantage. Your identity is your leverage, your differentiation, and your greatest advantage in the sponsorship and UGC world.

"The Moment Leila Transformed Her Image"

Leila had been creating content for two years, posting sporadically about makeup, skincare, workout routines, and her favorite café drinks. She loved creating, but she never felt like she had a clear identity. Her feed looked like a scrapbook of random moments rather than a cohesive brand. She dreamed of landing sponsorships but felt invisible to companies. Every time she saw another creator announce a brand deal, she wondered what they had that she didn't. She assumed it was followers or luck, but deep down she knew something was missing from her own profile. One night, she reached out to a creator she admired, someone who consistently landed deals. She hoped for a small piece of advice, but what she received was something that changed everything. The creator told her gently but honestly that her content was good, but her identity was unclear. She said that brands couldn't understand who she was or why they should choose her. It wasn't about talent—it was about clarity.

The comment shook Leila more than she expected. She had always thought that content alone was enough, but now she realized she needed direction. She spent the next few days studying her own page from the perspective of a brand. She pretended she was a marketing manager scrolling through her feed. What would she see? She noticed that her photos and videos had no consistent tone. One post was high-energy, another was calm, one looked aesthetic, another looked rushed. Her editing style changed constantly. Her bio didn't say what she did. Her highlights were messy and outdated. She realized that her page didn't speak for her. It didn't communicate a clear lifestyle, message, or vibe. It didn't represent the version of her she wanted brands to see. This realization stung, but it also sparked something inside her—a determination to rebuild her identity with intention.

Leila started over mentally, not by deleting posts but by redefining who she wanted to be as a creator. She asked herself what content she truly loved creating, the content that made her happiest and felt the most natural. She noticed a pattern: every post that revolved around skincare, wellness, and calming routines felt effortless. She loved storytelling in a soft, soothing tone. Her most saved videos were her nighttime routines and morning rituals. This was her identity—it had always been there, hidden beneath inconsistent content. She decided to embrace this version of herself fully. She refined her color palette, choosing warm neutrals and natural lighting. She simplified her editing style to match a peaceful, minimalistic vibe. She created a new bio that clearly stated her niche. She reorganized her highlights into clean categories: skincare, wellness, routines, reviews. Suddenly, her profile felt intentional.

As she continued posting consistently within her new identity, something shifted. Her audience began commenting that her content felt soothing and inspiring. They said her routines helped them slow down and care for themselves. Her engagement grew—not in numbers, but in depth. People asked for recommendations, requested tutorials, and shared how her videos made them feel. Her identity was finally resonating, and people could feel it. One day, a clean beauty brand emailed her, saying they loved her aesthetic and wanted to collaborate. They told her that her page represented exactly the lifestyle their customers desired: calm, intentional, and wellness-focused. They offered her a paid partnership. This was her first sponsorship, and she realized it came not because she posted more but because she posted with clarity.

Over the next few months, brands began noticing her. A supplement company reached out. Then a candle brand. Then a loungewear company. They all said the same thing—they felt aligned with her vibe. Her identity had become her magnet. She no longer felt invisible because her content now communicated exactly who she was. She wasn't trying to be everything; she was trying to be herself consistently. And that made her valuable. As she built more partnerships, she improved her lighting, upgraded her microphone, practiced storytelling, and refined her editing. Brands noticed her growth and rewarded it with bigger deals.

Leila eventually landed a three-month campaign with a major skincare brand, something she once thought was impossible. When she asked the brand's creative director why they chose her, they told her that her identity was clear, consistent, and emotionally engaging. They said her content made people feel something. That was the moment she understood the truth: brands choose creators whose identities feel strong, aligned, and intentional. Her transformation didn't begin when she got her first deal—it began when she stopped posting randomly and started showing up as the creator she truly was. Her identity became her superpower, and it changed the entire direction of her creator journey

Chapter 4

Optimizing Your Instagram Profile for Brand Deals

Your Instagram profile is the storefront of your creator business, and brands analyze it with extreme attention before ever reaching out or responding to your pitch. To a brand, your profile reveals not only what you post but how you think, how you communicate, and how professionally you operate. Many creators sabotage their ability to land sponsorships because their profile is unclear, unpolished, inconsistent, or difficult to interpret. Brands are not going to spend time trying to decode who you are—they want immediate clarity. The moment a brand lands on your page, they must instantly understand your niche, your aesthetic, your message, and your value. If that clarity is missing, brands assume you are not ready for paid partnerships. That's why optimizing your profile is a strategic necessity; it turns your page into a brand-attracting asset rather than just a collection of posts. Your profile speaks for you before you ever speak to a brand, so it must be deliberately crafted to communicate professionalism, alignment, and influence.

The first element of optimization is your bio. Brands read your bio before they ever look at your content. Your bio should clearly state who you are and what you create. It should instantly identify your niche and communicate the lifestyle or value you represent. Many creators use vague or aesthetic bios that look pretty but say nothing, leaving brands confused. A strong bio uses clarity, not poetry. It signals that you are a creator with direction, intention, and purpose. Brands also look for an email address or a contact button in your bio. If your contact information is missing, brands often assume you are not serious or not open for business. When a brand is evaluating hundreds of creators, they prefer the ones who make communication easy. Your bio is one of the simplest ways to elevate your perceived professionalism and signal to brands that you are prepared for collaboration.

Next, brands examine your highlights. Highlights act as "mini-portfolios" and allow brands to scan your content categories quickly. Organized highlights with consistent covers communicate that you treat your page like a brand, not a hobby. Brands look for highlights covering your niche, previous collaborations, routines, reviews, lifestyle content, or transformations. They want to see if you can tell stories through multiple media formats. They also want to see whether your content is polished or chaotic. Clean highlight covers, clear labels, and relevant content instantly elevate your image. Poorly organized highlights or empty pages lower your value because they create uncertainty. Highlights should reinforce your identity and show brands what they can expect if they partner with you. They are not just for your audience—they are for brands evaluating your value.

Another major factor brands examine is your feed cohesion. Brands are not looking for perfection, but they are looking for consistency. They scan the first nine posts to understand your aesthetic, your tone, and your content style. They want to see whether your feed communicates a lifestyle or narrative that aligns with their brand. A consistent visual identity reassures brands that you produce predictable and professional-quality content. If your feed looks chaotic, with radically different styles, filters, tones, and themes, brands may hesitate because they can't predict what their sponsored content will look like. A cohesive feed builds trust. This doesn't mean every post must look identical; it means your content should have a recognizable style. This style becomes your creator signature, helping brands imagine their product within your world.

Brands also evaluate your Reels specifically. Reels have become the primary format that brands use for awareness, engagement, and conversions. When brands review your profile, they examine how you deliver hooks, transitions, voiceovers, product integrations, and storytelling. They analyze whether you speak clearly on camera, whether your pacing keeps attention, and whether your editing communicates professionalism. They look for confidence, clarity, and creativity. Even if you produce aesthetic content without speaking, brands evaluate whether your visuals are strong enough to carry a message. Your Reels act as your audition tapes. They show brands exactly what you can deliver. When your Reels demonstrate strong storytelling and clean editing, your value increases dramatically.

Your captions also influence brand perception. Creators often underestimate the power of captions, but brands read them carefully. Captions reveal your communication skills, your personality, your values, and your ability to influence. A brand wants to see whether you can explain a product naturally, whether your audience listens to your recommendations, and whether your writing aligns with their tone. Captions also demonstrate your understanding of storytelling, authenticity, and relationship-building. Captions that are too short, inconsistent, or impersonal weaken your identity. Captions that flow, connect, and educate strengthen your creator brand. Captions are not just words—they're reputation signals to brands evaluating your potential.

The final element of optimizing your profile is ensuring your page feels intentional, polished, and aligned with your creator identity. Brands want creators who feel like a natural extension of their marketing message. If your profile communicates clarity, purpose, and professionalism, brands feel confident investing in you. A strong profile makes brands think, "We want our product represented in this world." When you optimize your profile to highlight your aesthetic, your voice, your niche, and your message, you transform your Instagram from a personal feed into a professional creator brand. Your optimized profile becomes a silent salesperson working for you twenty-four hours a day, attracting deals you didn't even pitch for. When brands can immediately understand who you are and what you do, your value multiplies—and sponsorship opportunities follow naturally.

"The Profile That Changed Everything"

Carlos had been posting fitness content for over a year, but he couldn't understand why brands never reached out to him. He poured effort into every workout Reel, filmed with dedication, kept his captions motivational, and posted consistently. Yet his inbox remained empty. He assumed that maybe he wasn't good enough or that brands only worked with massive creators. One evening, frustrated and exhausted, he asked a fellow creator why he wasn't landing any deals. The creator glanced at his profile for only thirty seconds and then said something that stunned him: your content is great, but your profile is confusing. Carlos didn't know what that meant. His friend explained that brands needed clarity. They needed to know within seconds who he was, what he stood for, and what value he provided. His profile didn't communicate any of that. It looked like a mix of fitness, memes, personal posts, and random content. To a brand, it didn't look like a creator ready for partnerships. That night, Carlos realized he needed to rebuild his profile from the ground up.

The next morning, he studied his page the way a brand manager would. He saw the inconsistencies he had been blind to: an unclear bio, cluttered highlights, mismatched colors, outdated posts, and conflicting tones. He realized his page didn't look intentional or cohesive; it looked like a hobby, not a brand. If he wanted brands to take him seriously, he needed to present himself professionally. The first thing he changed was his bio. He rewrote it to clearly state that he was a fitness creator specializing in strength training, beginner-friendly workouts, and home fitness routines. With one rewrite, he created clarity that had been missing for a year. Then he reorganized his highlights, deleting old, irrelevant clips and creating clean covers that matched his aesthetic. He created categories that a brand could instantly understand: workouts, routines, results, meals, reviews, and transformation. His page already felt more polished.

Once he cleaned up his highlights, he began focusing on his feed. He noticed that some posts felt serious and professional, but others felt chaotic and random. He realized that brands needed predictability—they needed to know what their product would look like in his hands. So he studied creators he admired and analyzed what made their feeds feel cohesive. It wasn't about perfection; it was about consistency. So he began choosing a color style for his edits, a tone for his captions, and a familiar structure for his workout Reels. He posted more intentionally, focusing on angles, transitions, and pacing. After a few weeks, his feed transformed into a clear fitness aesthetic that reflected his identity. For the first time, he felt like he had a brand, not just a page.

As his profile improved, his audience responded differently. People commented that his page felt more professional, more inspiring, more educational. They saved his posts at higher rates. His profile visits increased. His confidence grew. Still, he had no idea whether brands would notice—until one day, they did. A supplement company reached out to him for a small paid collaboration. They told him they loved the clarity of his profile and appreciated how easy it was to see his niche and aesthetic. They said his page looked like the type of creator their customers listened to. That email felt like validation for the months of hard work he had put into rebuilding his identity.

The sponsorship went smoothly, and the brand posted positive feedback. Soon after, a fitness equipment company contacted him. Then a wellness brand. Then a clothing company. Each of them mentioned the same thing: his profile was clean, intentional, and aligned with their marketing message. They felt confident working with him because his page communicated professionalism before he ever said a word. His optimized profile became his silent ambassador. It attracted opportunities without him pitching. It built trust before brands ever messaged him. It turned him from a frustrated creator into a rising fitness influencer with a growing roster of collaborations.

Months later, Carlos looked back at his old profile and barely recognized the person behind it. He realized that he had always been talented, but his presentation was holding him back. Once he redefined his identity visually and emotionally, everything changed. His profile became a magnet for deals, not because he gained millions of followers, but because he finally communicated who he was with clarity. The transformation taught him a powerful truth: your content may tell your story, but your profile sells your value. And once he optimized it, the world finally saw what he had to offer.

Chapter 5

Creating Portfolio Content That Attracts Paid Deals

One of the most powerful ways to attract paid brand deals—especially when you're still growing—is to create portfolio content that looks like sponsored work before brands ever hire you. Many creators wait for brands to contact them before producing high-quality product videos, testimonials, lifestyle shots, or educational content featuring items they already use. But brands don't choose creators randomly; they choose creators who already demonstrate the ability to represent products in a compelling, aesthetic, and conversion-friendly way. When brands review your page, they ask themselves a simple question: Can this creator make our product look good? If the answer isn't immediately clear from your content, they move on. The most successful creators build a portfolio intentionally, crafting content that mirrors the exact style of sponsored videos brands pay for. This establishes your capability, increases your perceived professionalism, and positions you as a brand partner even before you land your first paid collaboration.

Portfolio content is not about promoting brands for free. It is practice material, proof of concept, and a visual résumé rolled into one. When you create content using products you already own—skincare, tech, clothing, food, supplements, beauty tools, lifestyle items—you demonstrate your ability to integrate products naturally into your niche. Brands care far more about your skill than about whether the content is sponsored. When they see that you can showcase a product in a way that feels organic, engaging, and visually appealing, they trust you to do the same for them. Your portfolio becomes the evidence they need. It also signals that you understand the structure of product content: clear hooks, clean editing, storytelling, call-to-action style messaging, and a smooth blend between information and emotion. When your page already contains this type of content, brands feel more confident reaching out because you've already proven you can deliver.

To create compelling portfolio content, you must think like a brand. Brands want videos that stop the scroll, demonstrate their product clearly, and evoke a specific feeling. Your content should show not only what a product is but why it matters and how it fits into everyday life. Instead of holding the product up with stiff showcasing, you focus on lifestyle integration: applying a skincare serum in your routine, using a fitness tool during a workout, wearing an outfit while walking outside, showing a supplement in your morning ritual, or integrating a piece of tech into a daily setup. This kind of narrative-based content is what makes brands feel emotionally connected to your style. They begin to visualize their product in your world. That visualization often leads to outreach. When a brand sees you produce content that matches their marketing style—whether clean, cozy, energetic, luxury, or minimal—they categorize you as a creator who "gets it." And that drastically increases your chances of being hired.

Another important aspect of portfolio content is diversity of format. Brands evaluate creators not just on aesthetics but on versatility. They want to know whether you can create lifestyle videos, how-to tutorials, unboxings, voiceovers, problem-solution narratives, aesthetic b-roll montages, and talking-to-camera explanations. When your portfolio demonstrates multiple formats, brands trust that you can adapt to their specific needs. This is especially important for UGC creators, because brands often require content for various purposes: ads, product pages, emails, TikTok, and Instagram Reels. A versatile creator becomes more valuable because they can deliver a broader range of assets. When brands see variety in your portfolio, they understand that you can meet multiple deliverable types. This positions you as a multi-dimensional creator rather than someone who only excels in one format.

The quality of your portfolio content communicates your professionalism. Brands notice whether your lighting is clean, your audio is clear, your editing is smooth, and your pacing matches modern attention spans. They evaluate whether your transitions are sharp, your camera movements intentional, and your visuals aligned with your identity. The more polished your content appears, the higher your perceived value—and the higher your rates can be. You do not need expensive equipment; brands care more about storytelling and clarity than cinematic perfection. What matters is your intentionality. Brands want creators who understand the art of product representation, and your portfolio tells them whether you have mastered these fundamentals. When your content feels thoughtful and well-crafted, brands feel confident putting their marketing budget into your hands.

Finally, portfolio content establishes momentum. The more product-focused content you create, the more comfortable you become with showcasing products, telling stories, and communicating benefits naturally. This confidence shines through on camera and makes you a more compelling creator. Brands gravitate toward creators who look comfortable in their skin, confident in their storytelling, and clear in their purpose. Portfolio content builds this skill set and signals to brands that you are ready to operate professionally. It shows that you're not waiting for opportunities—you are creating them. This proactive energy attracts sponsorships, because brands prefer creators who treat partnerships seriously and approach content with intentionality. Your portfolio becomes your calling card, your audition reel, and your silent proof of professionalism. When you intentionally craft a portfolio that mirrors the style brands are already paying for, your chances of landing paid sponsorships increase dramatically.

"The Videos That Caught Their Eye"

Jasmine had been creating beauty content for months, but she always felt like she was stuck in the early stages of her creator journey. She loved filming GRWM videos, sharing product recommendations, and posting simple skincare routines, but no matter how much effort she put in, brands rarely noticed her. She envied other creators who seemed to land sponsorships effortlessly, even with smaller followings. One day, while scrolling through content from creators she admired, she noticed something she had never paid attention to before. Every creator receiving brand deals already had videos that looked like sponsored content—even before they were sponsored. Their pages were filled with polished tutorials, clean product shots, aesthetic b-roll, and lifestyle integrations. It suddenly made sense: brands weren't hiring them because they had deals—they were getting deals because they created content that brands could imagine sponsoring. That realization changed everything for Jasmine.

Inspired, she decided to create her first true "portfolio video." She chose a serum she already loved, cleared her space, turned on a small lamp for cozy lighting, and recorded herself going through her nighttime skincare routine. She filmed close-ups of the product, soft shots of her applying it, and gentle transitions between steps. She recorded a calm voiceover explaining why she liked the serum and how it made her skin feel. For the first time, she approached content not as a creator hoping for views but as a professional demonstrating what she could offer to brands. When she edited the video, she added smooth movements, warm tones, and soft music. It felt different—elevated, intentional, polished. When she posted it, her audience reacted strongly, saving it, commenting on the aesthetics, and asking questions. But the most surprising reaction didn't come from her followers; it came from a brand.

Three days later, she received a message from a skincare company she had admired for years. They said they loved her video style, especially her warm visuals and gentle voiceovers. They said her content aligned perfectly with their brand and asked if she would be interested in creating UGC content for them. Jasmine stared at the message in disbelief. It was the first time a brand had taken her seriously, and it happened because she created something that showed them her potential. She accepted the offer, created two videos for the brand, and realized how powerful her portfolio could be. The collaboration wasn't just a milestone—it was proof that her new approach worked.

Encouraged, Jasmine began producing more portfolio-style content. She created an unboxing video for a moisturizer, a routine showcasing her favorite SPF, a transformation clip comparing before-and-after results, and a calming reel about self-care. She used products she already owned and loved. This gave her an authentic voice, and her content reflected her genuine experience. Her confidence grew with each video. Her storytelling became clearer, her editing smoother, and her aesthetic more refined. Her profile transformed into a cohesive portfolio that visually communicated her value. She wasn't waiting anymore—she was building her own momentum.

As she grew more consistent, brands began reaching out more frequently. A clean-beauty brand contacted her for a small campaign. A haircare brand discovered her through one of her product tutorials. A wellness company saw her routine video and wanted something similar. Each brand mentioned the same thing: her portfolio content felt professional, compelling, and emotionally aligned with their message. Jasmine realized that brands were not hiring her for her follower count—they were hiring her for her style, her storytelling, and her ability to make products feel meaningful. Her portfolio had become her audition, and it was opening doors she once thought were out of reach.

Months later, Jasmine landed her biggest deal yet—a three-month partnership with a major global skincare brand. They told her that they discovered her through her early portfolio videos, the ones she created when she decided to shift her mindset. They said her content felt authentic, polished, and persuasive. When she delivered the first video for the campaign, the brand's marketing team told her it was some of the best UGC they had received all year. Jasmine realized that her transformation began the moment she stopped hoping for opportunities and started creating content that reflected the creator she wanted to become. Her portfolio became her turning point and the reason brands finally saw her potential.

Chapter 6

Crafting Your Media Kit & Rate Card

A media kit is one of the most powerful tools a creator can have when pursuing Instagram sponsorships and UGC deals. It is the professional package that tells brands exactly who you are, what you offer, and why you are worth paying. Many creators underestimate the importance of a media kit, thinking it's only for influencers with large followings, but in reality, even micro and nano creators benefit from having one. A well-designed media kit communicates professionalism, clarity, confidence, and preparedness—qualities that brands value more than follower count. It helps you position yourself as a serious creator, not just someone casually posting content. When brands see a polished media kit, they immediately think of you differently: as someone organized, capable, and ready to deliver results. Your media kit becomes your silent salesperson, showcasing your identity before you ever speak to a brand.

The first essential element of a strong media kit is your creator identity summary. This brief overview should communicate your niche, message, tone, and content style. It tells brands who you are and why your presence matters. Brands don't want a generic creator—they want someone with a defined point of view and a recognizable style. This summary should express your value through emotion and clarity. For example, if you are a wellness creator, your summary might speak to your calming aesthetic, your focus on intentional routines, and your ability to make audiences feel grounded. If you're a fitness creator, it may highlight your motivational tone and your knowledge of training principles. Your identity summary sets the tone for the rest of the media kit. It shows brands that you understand yourself, your audience, and your purpose as a creator.

Next, your media kit must present your audience analytics. Even if your following is small, brands want to understand who your audience is and how they engage with your content. They look for demographic information such as age, gender, location, and interests. They examine engagement rates, reach, impressions, and content formats. This doesn't need to be hyper-detailed, but it should provide a snapshot of your platform's behavior. Even if your numbers feel modest, brands appreciate transparency because it helps them match creators with campaigns more accurately. Many creators fear sharing analytics because they feel their numbers aren't impressive enough, but brands care more about alignment and quality than raw metrics. Your analytics show that you understand your audience and their needs, which increases your appeal.

After your analytics, the most important part of your media kit is your portfolio showcase. This is where you highlight your top-performing content, examples of product videos, testimonials, tutorials, reels, lifestyle visuals, and previous brand collaborations if you have any. Even if you don't have past sponsorships, your portfolio content—created using products you already own—will serve as proof of your skill. Brands want to see your storytelling, editing style, lighting, hooks, and transitions. This section should show your best work and reflect the style you want to be hired for. If you want wellness brands, showcase wellness content. If you want fashion brands, highlight outfits and styling clips. Brands choose creators who already produce the type of content they envision for their campaigns. Your portfolio section helps them visualize your work representing their product.

Another critical part of your media kit is your rate card. Many creators struggle with pricing because they fear charging too much or too little. But brands expect you to have clear rates, and having a rate card shows confidence and professionalism. Your rate card should outline your pricing for different deliverables such as Reels, stories, carousels, whitelisting rights, usage rights, UGC videos, and package deals. It should be structured clearly, with straightforward language. Rates can vary depending on niche, experience, audience size, and content quality, but what matters most is that your pricing feels intentional and consistent. Rates are a starting point; brands may negotiate, but without a rate card, you appear unprepared. A well-structured rate card signals that you take your business seriously.

Your media kit should also include a section about brand alignment—your values, your aesthetic, your mission, and the types of brands you enjoy partnering with. Brands want to work with creators who genuinely fit their identity and customers. When you clearly communicate your alignment, you make their decision easier. You can describe your approach to storytelling, the emotions you evoke, and your goals as a creator. This section helps brands feel confident that you can represent them authentically. It also subtly communicates your standards and boundaries, showing that you choose collaborations thoughtfully. Brands prefer creators who know themselves and their message because it leads to more authentic content.

The final element of your media kit is your contact information. This may seem small, but it matters. Brands want to see a clear email address, your name, your location (general region, not specific address), and any additional platforms you want to share. Contact clarity builds trust. When a brand reviews hundreds of creators, they choose the ones who make communication easy. A professional email address, not tied to unrelated usernames or casual handles, enhances your credibility. Once your media kit is complete, it becomes a powerful tool that elevates your perceived value instantly. It shows brands that you treat your creator journey like a business. When you combine a polished media kit with a strong portfolio, brands see you as someone worth investing in. Your media kit becomes your entry point to higher rates, better deals, and long-term partnerships. It turns uncertainty into clarity and positions you as a professional creator ready to collaborate at a high level.

"The Kit That Changed the Conversation"

Alyssa had been creating lifestyle and wellness content for almost a year, and although she loved the creative process, she constantly struggled with one thing: brands didn't take her seriously. They responded slowly, negotiated aggressively, or ignored her entirely. Even when she managed to secure a small collaboration, she felt undervalued, underpaid, and overwhelmed. She couldn't understand why brands didn't seem to recognize her potential. Her content was consistent, aesthetically pleasing, and engaging, but the way brands treated her made her feel like she had no authority. That changed when a more experienced creator offered her unexpected advice after noticing her frustration. She told Alyssa that the way she presented herself—through her communications, profile, and materials—was affecting how brands perceived her professionalism. She asked Alyssa a question that stung: "Do you have a media kit?" Alyssa admitted she didn't. Her friend simply replied that the moment she created one, everything would change.

That night, Alyssa researched media kits and realized she had been operating without a vital part of the creator business toolkit. She gathered her analytics, reviewed her best-performing content, analyzed her audience demographics, and wrote a summary of who she was as a creator. She described her niche as wellness routines, self-care strategies, and simple lifestyle improvements. She highlighted the calming aesthetic of her videos and the emotional connection her audience often expressed in the comments. She chose warm colors and clean layout designs that matched her brand identity. Creating the media kit forced her to see herself differently—as a business, not just a hobby creator. She felt a sense of clarity and empowerment she had never experienced before.

When she finished her media kit, she created her rate card. She had never written down her rates before; she always improvised when brands asked, which made her feel unprepared and insecure. But now, writing her rates with confidence made her feel solid and professional. She priced each deliverable—Reels, stories, carousels, usage rights, and UGC videos—based on her time, skill, and niche market. For the first time, her pricing felt intentional. It felt like a statement of her worth. She included examples of her top-performing content, especially videos that demonstrated her soothing tone and intentional storytelling. She added testimonials from her audience and screenshots of her analytics. When she looked at the final media kit, she felt proud. It looked like the kind of kit a serious creator would present. It looked like her.

A few days later, a wellness brand reached out, asking for her rates. Instead of responding nervously or delaying her reply, she confidently sent her media kit. The difference in the brand's response was immediate. They replied professionally, respected her pricing, and asked a series of thoughtful questions. They treated her like a partner, not an amateur. She realized the media kit had changed the entire tone of the interaction. She was no longer negotiating from a place of insecurity; she was presenting herself as a professional. The brand hired her for a paid collaboration without hesitation. It was the smoothest negotiation she had ever experienced.

As she continued sending her media kit to brands, the pattern repeated itself. Brands responded faster. They respected her rates. They asked fewer basic questions because her media kit already answered them. Some brands even complimented her presentation and said it made her stand out. One company told her that her kit was more impressive than some full-time influencers they had worked with. That comment alone made her realize how far she had come. Her media kit elevated her value before she ever created a piece of content.

Months later, Alyssa secured a long-term partnership with a luxury wellness brand—something she once thought was out of reach. When the brand's marketing director explained why they selected her, they mentioned her media kit specifically. They said it was clear, elegant, aligned with their aesthetic, and demonstrated her professionalism. They said it showed she understood the business side of the creator industry, which made her a reliable long-term partner. Alyssa realized that creating her media kit didn't just help brands see her differently—it helped her see herself differently. It clarified her identity, strengthened her confidence, and transformed her creator journey. The kit didn't just change conversations; it changed her entire future as a creator.

Chapter 7

Mastering Brand Outreach: Pitches That Get Responses

Brand outreach is one of the most powerful skills a creator can develop, yet it is also the most misunderstood. Many creators assume that outreach means desperately begging brands for opportunities, but the reality is far different. Outreach is not about asking for favors; it is about initiating professional conversations with companies whose marketing you can genuinely enhance. Brands do not see outreach as annoying or intrusive. In fact, many expect creators to reach out because they constantly need new content, new faces, and new voices for their campaigns. The issue is not outreach itself—it's the way creators approach it. Poorly written messages, unclear proposals, weak positioning, and casual tone cause most outreach to fail. When you understand how to structure a pitch that resonates with brands, your outreach transforms from ignored messages into meaningful collaborations that pay well and lead to long-term partnerships.

The first step in effective outreach is understanding your value before you message any brand. Many creators approach outreach with insecurity, hoping a brand will "give them a chance." But brands don't give chances—they make investments. They invest in creators who understand their own worth, who can explain why their content is beneficial, and who can articulate what they bring to the table. Before you send a pitch, you must be clear about your niche, identity, storytelling style, and the emotions your content evokes. This self-awareness allows you to communicate your value concisely. When a brand senses confidence and clarity, they listen. When they sense self-doubt, they disengage. The strongest pitches come from creators who understand exactly why their content matters.

The second pillar of successful outreach is personalization. Brands can tell immediately when a creator sends mass messages that are copied and pasted hundreds of times. Those pitches feel generic, impersonal, and uninspired. Brands want to feel chosen. They want to know why you picked them specifically and how your content aligns with their mission. Before contacting a brand, study their aesthetic, their messaging, their product benefits, and their target customer. Look at their recent marketing campaigns. Look at the tone of their Instagram feed. When you reference these details in your pitch, the brand feels seen and understood. They realize you didn't send a random message—you sent an intentional, thoughtful proposal rooted in genuine interest.

The third key to outreach is clarity. Brands receive countless messages daily from creators who ramble, overshare, or send paragraphs that do not get to the point. Brand managers do not have time to read long, unfocused messages. Your pitch must be concise, structured, and easy to understand. A strong pitch communicates who you are, what you create, why you love the brand, and what type of collaboration you're interested in. It should not include your life story, your entire creative history, or technical jargon. Brands want simplicity. They want to know whether you're a good fit, what you're proposing, and why they should continue the conversation. When your pitch feels clean and intentional, brands pay attention.

Another major factor in pitch success is demonstrating your understanding of the brand's goals. Brands hire creators for different reasons: brand awareness, conversions, lifestyle representation, product tutorials, or user-generated content for ads. The more your pitch reflects their objectives, the more persuasive it becomes. For example, if a brand recently launched a new product, referencing it shows awareness. If a brand focuses on sustainability, aligning your message with their values creates connection. If a brand's marketing emphasizes emotional storytelling, highlighting your storytelling strength resonates deeply. Outreach works when you position yourself as a solution—not a random applicant.

Timing also plays a fundamental role. Many creators send one message and never follow up, assuming the brand isn't interested. But most brand managers are overwhelmed with admin tasks, emails, and campaigns. They often miss messages, forget to respond, or plan to reply later and never do. Following up is a normal part of outreach and shows professionalism, not desperation. A follow-up message sent with clarity and confidence dramatically increases your chances of receiving a response. Creators who follow up consistently land far more deals than creators who send a single message and give up.

Finally, the energy behind your outreach determines how it is received. Brands can sense the difference between empowerment and insecurity. Outreach rooted in confidence, clarity, and genuine admiration for the brand comes across as professional and appealing. Outreach rooted in desperation or fear comes across as weak and unconvincing. When you pitch from the mindset that you are offering value—not requesting validation—you change the entire dynamic. You become a partner, not a petitioner. Mastering outreach means mastering the tone, structure, clarity, and psychology behind your pitch. Once you understand these elements, outreach stops feeling intimidating and becomes one of the most reliable ways to generate brand deals consistently, predictably, and sustainably.

"The Message That Opened Every Door"

Nina had always been afraid to message brands. She felt small, inexperienced, and invisible compared to the creators she admired. Every time she thought about sending a pitch, she convinced herself that brands would laugh at her tiny following or ignore her entirely. But after months of waiting for opportunities that never came, she realized that if she didn't take initiative, nothing would change. Her breakthrough came unexpectedly while watching a behind-the-scenes interview with a brand manager. He explained that brands love when creators reach out because it helps them discover new talent. That sentence shifted something inside her. She realized she wasn't intruding—she was presenting an opportunity. And so, one afternoon, with her heart racing, she decided it was time to craft her first pitch.

But instead of writing out of fear, Nina wanted to write with intention. She reviewed her content and asked herself what made her videos stand out. She noticed that people often commented on how comforting her voiceovers were and how her aesthetic made them feel calm and inspired. She realized that her strength wasn't her follower count—it was her ability to create emotion. With that clarity, she began studying a wellness brand she admired. She looked at their colors, their messaging, the kind of customers they targeted, and the overall feel of their page. Their brand tone felt soothing, grounded, and mindful. She realized she aligned with them more than she had ever realized. For the first time, she felt like she belonged in the brand's world.

She wrote the pitch carefully. She didn't try to impress them with numbers or grand claims. She simply shared who she was, why their brand resonated with her, and how her content could support their message. She made the message warm, confident, and concise. After she sent it, she expected silence. Instead, the brand responded within two hours. They thanked her for the thoughtful message and asked to see her media kit. Nina felt overwhelmed with emotion—her message wasn't ignored. It wasn't dismissed. It was welcomed. A few days later, they hired her for a paid collaboration. It was her very first sponsorship, and it happened because she finally understood that outreach wasn't begging—it was offering value.

Encouraged by her success, Nina began reaching out to more brands. This time, she approached outreach with strategy. She researched each company, learned their tone, studied their recent campaigns, and crafted personalized pitches that highlighted her alignment with their messaging. She wasn't sending generic messages; she was building genuine connections. She started receiving more responses. Some brands asked for her rates. Others complimented her aesthetic. A few said they had already seen her content and were glad she reached out. Each message boosted her confidence. She realized that brand managers were human beings, not gatekeepers. They appreciated authenticity, clarity, and professionalism.

One of Nina's biggest turning points came when she pitched a respected wellness brand known for working with larger influencers. She assumed her message wouldn't matter to them, but she had grown stronger through her previous successes. She personalized the pitch deeply, referencing a recent product launch and aligning it with her morning routine aesthetic. Weeks passed, and she heard nothing. Old Nina would have given up, but the new Nina followed up politely. The brand responded the same day. They apologized for missing her first message and expressed excitement about working with her. Her follow-up reopened a door she thought was closed.

The campaign that followed became her most successful to date. The brand loved her content so much that they extended the collaboration from a single post into a two-month partnership. Their marketing director later revealed something that shocked her: they received dozens of pitches weekly, but her outreach stood out because it felt thoughtful, aligned, and professional. She hadn't relied on numbers—she relied on clarity and authenticity. That insight changed her mind forever about outreach. It wasn't about follower count; it was about approach, tone, and purpose.

Months later, Nina became known for her ability to secure deals consistently. Other creators began asking her how she landed so many partnerships. She always answered with the same truth: the pitch changed everything. Not because it was perfect, but because it came from confidence and genuine alignment. Her fear had been replaced with certainty. She finally understood that brands weren't unreachable giants—they were simply waiting for the right message from the right creator. And once she found her voice, every message she sent became a doorway to new opportunities and a new future she had once believed was out of reach.

Chapter 8

Negotiating Rates, Deliverables & Usage Rights

Negotiation is one of the most misunderstood yet essential skills in the creator industry. Many creators enter conversations with brands feeling grateful just to be noticed, and this gratitude often comes at the cost of their worth. Brands expect negotiation. They budget for it. They plan for it. And they rarely offer their full budget in the first message. Yet most creators accept the initial offer—afraid that pushing back will make the brand walk away. The truth is that professional negotiation is not confrontational; it is strategic, respectful, and mutually beneficial. Brands value creators who understand how to negotiate because it demonstrates professionalism, confidence, and business awareness. When you negotiate, you are not demanding more than you deserve—you are ensuring the partnership reflects your talent, your time, and your expertise.

Understanding your value is the first step in negotiation. Your rates are not just random numbers—they reflect your niche, your content style, your editing skills, your audience's trust, the time required to produce assets, and the emotional connection you create through storytelling. Rates also reflect the type of deliverable. A Reel, for example, involves ideation, scripting, filming, editing, revisions, and multiple rounds of feedback. A Story set requires less editing but still demands time and creativity. Usage rights amplify your rates further, especially when brands want to use your content as paid ads or on their website. When you recognize how much labor, skill, and creativity goes into each piece of content, you understand that negotiation is not optional—it is essential.

One of the most important aspects of negotiation is separating deliverables from usage rights. Many creators mistakenly include usage rights in their base rate without charging separately, but usage rights are one of the most valuable components in a deal. When a brand wants to use your content on their website, social media, email campaigns, or advertising platforms, your content becomes a marketing asset—often generating thousands or even millions of impressions. Usage rights allow them to profit from your creativity beyond your personal page. Because of this, usage rights should always cost extra. Creators who understand this earn far higher income than those who treat usage rights casually. Negotiation begins with understanding what is included and what requires additional licensing.

Another essential factor is clarity. When negotiating, you must clearly define the deliverables, deadlines, revision expectations, usage terms, and payment details. Vagueness leads to confusion, scope creep, and underpayment. Creators often feel uncomfortable setting boundaries, but clarity is a sign of professionalism. Brands appreciate creators who define expectations from the beginning. This clarity shows that you are organized, dependable, and experienced. When you establish the framework early, negotiation becomes smoother and more predictable. Instead of guessing, both parties understand the terms clearly.

Confidence plays a major role in negotiation success. Brands can sense when a creator communicates from insecurity. They can also sense when a creator communicates from strength. Confident communication does not mean arrogance—it means stating your rates calmly, explaining your reasoning, and maintaining a tone of collaboration. Confidence makes negotiation feel natural instead of stressful. Brands respect creators who understand their worth and communicate professionally. Confidence also prevents you from accepting low offers out of fear. When a brand sees that you negotiate with clarity and composure, they are more willing to adjust their offer. Many brands even increase their budgets when they encounter a creator who communicates professionally, because they trust that the quality of the work will match the professionalism.

Negotiation also requires flexibility—not in lowering your worth but in presenting options. Brands appreciate choices. Offering alternative packages or revised structures allows both parties to reach a comfortable agreement without compromising the integrity of your work. Flexibility demonstrates that you understand business relationships and that you can adapt your offer without undervaluing yourself. It makes negotiation feel collaborative rather than confrontational. Brands are far more likely to accept a proposal when they feel included in the decision-making process.

Finally, negotiation ends with documentation. Every agreement with a brand—whether small or large—should be documented. Contracts protect both you and the brand. They outline deliverables, rates, usage terms, timelines, revisions, and payment deadlines. Many creators avoid contracts because they feel intimidated by legal terms, but contracts are simply clarity in writing. They empower you, protect your time, and ensure that the partnership unfolds smoothly. Understanding how to negotiate, document agreements, and communicate professionally elevates your value dramatically. Negotiation is not a barrier—it is the bridge that transforms you from an amateur creator into a respected professional with long-term earning potential.

"The Negotiation That Transformed Her Career"

Sofia had always been the kind of creator who accepted whatever brands offered her. She felt grateful for every opportunity, so when a company proposed a rate, she said yes without hesitation. She never questioned whether it was fair or whether she deserved more. Deep down, she feared that if she pushed back, the offer would disappear. She told herself she didn't have enough followers or experience to negotiate. But the truth was that she lacked confidence, not ability. Everything changed when a wellness brand reached out with a campaign that felt like a dream. They loved her storytelling style and wanted her to create two videos for their launch. Sofia was thrilled—until she saw the offer. They proposed a rate far below industry standards. She felt torn between her excitement and the nagging feeling that she was being undervalued.

For the first time, she paused before responding. She remembered a piece of advice she had heard: "Brands expect negotiation. You're not asking for more—you're asking for fair value." With trembling hands, she drafted a message explaining her rates and why the deliverables required more time, creativity, and licensing fees than their initial offer reflected. She wrote with respect but also with a firmness she had never shown before. Her finger hovered over the send button, her heart pounding. Finally, she sent it. She expected the brand to vanish. Instead, fifteen minutes later, they responded. They thanked her for her professionalism, acknowledged her reasoning, and agreed to her rate without hesitation. Sofia sat in shock. She had spent years underpricing herself for fear of rejection, only to discover that negotiation wasn't a risk—it was expected.

When the campaign began, the brand provided clear instructions and trusted her creative vision. She delivered two videos that quickly became some of the brand's top-performing pieces of content. After they saw the results, they requested additional usage rights to run the videos as ads. In the past, Sofia would have agreed for free, thinking it was simply part of the partnership. But now she understood her worth. She explained that usage rights required an additional licensing fee. The brand agreed again without pushback. She realized that her lack of negotiation had been costing her not only money but respect. The brand now saw her as a professional, not just a creator excited for attention.

Months passed, and Sofia's confidence grew with each negotiation. She learned how to separate deliverables from usage rights, how to politely decline low offers, and how to present options when brands needed flexibility. She noticed that the brands she negotiated with treated her differently—they communicated with more respect, provided clearer briefs, and paid timely. Negotiation had strengthened her identity. It didn't push brands away; it attracted the right ones.

Her biggest turning point came when a luxury skincare brand contacted her. They were launching a new line and wanted creators who could deliver high-end visuals. Sofia created a stunning concept proposal and sent her rates. The brand responded with a number half of what she quoted. Old Sofia would have accepted instantly. But the new Sofia calmly explained her value, the time required, the creative direction involved, and the usage rights needed. She offered a revised package that aligned with their budget without diminishing her worth. The brand took two days to respond. When they finally did, they accepted her full rate and agreed to a three-month partnership. They explained that her professionalism during negotiation proved she was the right creator for their campaign.

After the partnership ended, the brand's marketing director sent her a message she would never forget. He told her that her negotiation style showed maturity and respect for her craft. He said they preferred working with creators who understood their value because it made collaborations smoother and more impactful. That message validated every moment of doubt she had overcome. Negotiation hadn't just increased her income—it had elevated her identity, transformed her career, and shown her that being paid fairly was not a luxury; it was a standard.

Sofia realized that creators lose far more by staying silent than they ever lose by negotiating. Her entire career changed the moment she decided to advocate for herself. She learned that negotiation wasn't a battle—it was a conversation between two professionals seeking alignment. And that realization unlocked opportunities, confidence, and partnerships she once believed were out of reach.

Chapter 9

Delivering High-Impact Sponsored Content

Delivering high-impact sponsored content is one of the most influential factors in building a long-term, profitable creator career. Many creators focus heavily on landing brand deals but underestimate how crucial the delivery phase is. When you produce content that exceeds expectations, brands take notice. They remember you. They come back. They increase budgets. They extend contracts. They refer you to other brands. Your delivery is not simply the fulfillment of a contract—it is your opportunity to demonstrate your professionalism, creativity, consistency, and value in a way that sets you apart from other creators. The content you produce becomes the strongest form of marketing for your future partnerships because your results speak louder than any pitch ever could.

The first key to delivering high-impact content is understanding the brand's objective. Brands pay creators for different reasons, and your sponsored content must align with their goal. Some campaigns are focused on awareness, while others are centered on conversions, storytelling, education, lifestyle integration, or UGC content for ads. When you understand the purpose of the campaign, you can craft your content with intentionality. If the brand's goal is emotional connection, your content should evoke feeling. If the goal is education, your content must provide clarity. If the goal is demonstrating results, your visuals must be clear and honest. High-impact content is never random; it is strategically designed to fulfill the brand's vision while still fitting your voice.

Another crucial element is maintaining your authenticity. Brands hire creators precisely because their audiences trust them. If sponsored content feels forced, unnatural, or overly scripted, viewers disengage—and brands notice. High-impact sponsored content blends seamlessly into your existing style. It should feel like your voice, your aesthetic, and your routine, not a departure from your normal content. The strongest sponsored pieces are the ones where the audience does not even realize it is sponsored until the call-to-action appears. The brand receives quality representation, and your audience receives genuine value. Maintaining this balance is a hallmark of powerful creators.

High-impact content also requires strong storytelling. Every piece of sponsored content—whether a Reel, carousel, or Story—should have a beginning, middle, and end. The beginning captures attention with a hook. The middle provides value, emotion, or transformation. The end ties everything together with a clear purpose. Storytelling is what transforms a simple product shot into a compelling narrative. When you tell a story, you give context, meaning, and emotional resonance. This is what drives results for brands. They don't want creators who simply display products—they want creators who integrate products meaningfully into their content. When you elevate your storytelling, you elevate your income.

Another sign of high-impact delivery is attention to detail. Brands notice when you take the time to refine your lighting, adjust your framing, choose intentional music, edit transitions smoothly, and craft thoughtful voiceovers. They notice when you submit content early, when you provide multiple angles, when you show creativity rather than minimal effort. Details communicate passion and professionalism. Brands are more likely to extend partnerships with creators who deliver polished, purposeful work. When you consistently produce high-quality content, you set yourself apart in an industry where many creators cut corners or rush deliverables.

Timeliness also plays a major role in brand perception. Turning content in on time—or early—signals responsibility and reliability. Brands often work with strict campaign deadlines, and late submissions can jeopardize an entire launch. When you deliver promptly, brands see you as trustworthy. They feel confident entrusting you with larger projects in the future. Timeliness is a small detail that has massive influence on how brands perceive your professionalism.

Finally, high-impact delivery includes openness to collaboration. This means being receptive to feedback, revisions, and adjustments. Brands appreciate creators who maintain artistic integrity while also being flexible enough to incorporate changes. This does not mean allowing brands to micromanage your creativity. Instead, it means understanding that collaboration is a two-way street, and that small adjustments can elevate the final product without compromising your voice. When you master collaboration, brands view you as someone who is easy to work with—an invaluable quality. Delivering high-impact sponsored content requires intentionality, consistency, creativity, and professionalism. When you master these elements, you position yourself as a top-tier creator capable of building long-term partnerships and earning premium rates.

"When One Video Changed Everything"

Riley had always dreamed of landing a major brand deal, but she never imagined that the quality of her delivery—not her pitch—would be what transformed her career. She had secured her first few collaborations earlier in the year, and while she completed them, she treated them like simple tasks rather than professional projects. She delivered what she thought the brands wanted, but she didn't put her full creative energy into the work. The content was acceptable but not memorable. The brands thanked her, posted the videos, and moved on. No one offered extensions or higher-paying opportunities. She assumed this was normal until the day she received a message from a prominent wellness brand offering her a chance to create one sponsored Reel for their new morning supplement. Riley felt excited but nervous. Something inside her told her that this collaboration needed to be different.

Instead of rushing, she decided to treat this project with the highest level of intention she had ever brought to her work. She studied the brand's aesthetic, their mission, and the storytelling style in their ads. She realized they focused on warm tones, calm energy, and emotionally resonant routines. She asked herself how she could create a video that felt true to her voice but also aligned with their brand. She planned a morning routine reel that showed her sunlight-filled kitchen, her quiet journaling time, and gentle product integration. She filmed multiple angles, took her time editing, recorded a soft voiceover, and refined the pacing until everything felt seamless. When she finished, the video felt like a piece of art rather than a sponsorship.

When she submitted the content, she expected the brand to request changes or adjustments. Instead, they replied immediately with a message she had never received before: they were blown away. They said her video exceeded their expectations, captured their brand identity flawlessly, and evoked a feeling they struggled to find in other creators' work. They asked if they could extend the collaboration and hire her for two additional videos. Riley couldn't believe what she was reading. Before this campaign, no brand had ever extended a partnership with her. But now, because she poured her creativity, effort, and storytelling into a single piece of content, everything changed.

The video performed incredibly well. The brand used it in their ads, and it outperformed several previous campaigns. They emailed Riley again to negotiate extended usage rights and asked if she would consider a long-term partnership for the next quarter. Riley realized, with a mix of gratitude and shock, that she had unlocked a new level in her creator career. Her delivery—not her following, not her pitch, not her analytics—was the reason. She understood for the first time that brands weren't simply paying for her audience; they were paying for her storytelling, her visuals, her ability to evoke a feeling. Her creativity had value far beyond what she had imagined.

As more brands saw her work through reposts and ads, they began contacting her. Within weeks, she tripled her inbound brand inquiries. A skincare brand reached out, saying her video with the wellness company made them feel something—and that they wanted the same feeling in their own campaign. A fitness brand admired her lighting and transitions. A mindfulness app praised her voiceover. Her single high-impact delivery became her strongest portfolio piece, and brands used it to evaluate her potential for future partnerships.

Months later, Riley looked back at the moment she decided to take the project seriously and realized that it marked the beginning of her evolution. She learned that being a creator was not about doing the minimum required—it was about creating content that reflected her identity and passion. She discovered that when she delivered high-impact content, brands treated her differently. They offered higher rates, clearer contracts, and long-term opportunities. One video changed the entire trajectory of her life. Through it, she understood a truth she would carry forever: when you deliver with excellence, your content becomes your greatest advocate, opening doors you didn't even know existed.

Chapter 10

Turning One-Off Deals Into Long-Term Partnerships

One-off brand deals can help creators earn money, but long-term partnerships are where true financial stability is built. Brands do not want to constantly search for new creators, onboard new personalities, and rebuild trust every month. They prefer working with creators who deliver quality, professionalism, and consistency—creators who make collaboration easy and aligned. When you transform a single campaign into a multi-month contract, you shift from unpredictable income to recurring revenue. Long-term partnerships also elevate your authority because brands promote you repeatedly, increasing your visibility, trust, and value in the creator economy. Turning one project into many is not luck—it is strategy, intention, and relationship-building.

The first key to earning long-term partnerships is exceeding expectations during the initial collaboration. Brands evaluate creators heavily during their first project together. They watch how you communicate, how timely you are, how closely you follow instructions, and how creatively you deliver. When you overdeliver—through thoughtful storytelling, clean visuals, fast communication, and polished editing—you demonstrate reliability. Reliability is rare, and brands reward it. Many creators produce average content and wonder why brands don't return. But brands return to creators who make them feel safe, supported, and understood. When you exceed expectations, you become memorable.

The second pillar of long-term collaboration is communication. Brands want creators who respond promptly, ask smart questions, and maintain professionalism. Communication builds trust, and trust is the foundation of business. If you consistently communicate clearly during your first project, brands feel comfortable hiring you again. They prefer creators who don't need micromanagement, who respect deadlines, and who keep the partnership smooth. When you send updates, confirm details, and show enthusiasm, directors feel connected to you. They begin to see you as part of their extended creative team rather than just another influencer for a one-off campaign.

Another essential component is demonstrating alignment with the brand's mission. Brands love creators who genuinely embody their values and aesthetic. When you choose collaborations that naturally fit your niche, your content feels authentic. This authenticity becomes attractive to brands seeking ongoing representation. If your aesthetic matches theirs consistently, you become an ideal long-term partner.

Brands are not looking for creators who fit only one campaign—they want creators who visually and emotionally match their long-term identity. When you align yourself intentionally with the right brands, your opportunities multiply.

Long-term partnerships also require strategic follow-up. Many creators finish a campaign and never speak to the brand again. This silence creates a weak connection. Instead, after delivering your final content, send a follow-up message expressing gratitude and openness to future projects. Remind the brand that you enjoyed working with them and that you would love to support upcoming launches or campaigns. If your previous content performed well, mention any analytics or positive audience feedback. Proactive communication demonstrates leadership and initiative. Brands remember creators who maintain relationships because it shows you value the partnership.

Offering ideas is another powerful way to extend collaborations. After completing a project, think creatively about how you could continue supporting the brand. Propose seasonal content, educational content, transformation videos, or long-term story series. Brands appreciate creators who think beyond the contract. When you present ideas aligned with their goals, you position yourself as a valuable partner rather than someone waiting to be hired. Idea-driven creators stand out because they make marketing teams' jobs easier.

Finally, professionalism determines your long-term earning potential. Brands want creators who respect contracts, deliver revisions gracefully, and accept feedback without ego. They want creators who treat partnerships as business relationships. Long-term collaborations depend heavily on trust, consistency, and quality. When you maintain your standards across every campaign, brands naturally gravitate toward you for future work. Turning one-off deals into ongoing partnerships is an art—an art rooted in quality, communication, alignment, initiative, and professionalism. When you master this art, your creator career becomes stable, profitable, and increasingly in demand.

"The Partnership She Never Expected"

Marina had worked with dozens of brands over her first year as a creator, but every collaboration seemed to end as quickly as it began. Brands thanked her, posted her content, and moved on. She envied creators who announced multi-month campaigns and long-term partnerships, wondering what they were doing that she wasn't. She delivered her content, met deadlines, and put effort into her work, but nothing extended beyond a single post. She eventually convinced herself that long-term opportunities were reserved for creators with giant followings or industry connections. That belief held until she collaborated with a small skincare company for what she assumed would be another one-time project.

From the beginning, Marina treated the collaboration differently. She loved the brand's mission, their clean ingredients, and their storytelling style. Instead of rushing through the content, she immersed herself in their world. She read their website, watched their past campaigns, and paid attention to their emotional tone. She wanted to reflect their identity in her content while staying true to her own style. When she created the video, she filmed multiple angles, crafted a soft voiceover, and wove their product into her morning routine. The video felt intimate—soft sunlight, quiet motion, and genuine care. It was her most thoughtful work yet.

She delivered the content early. She communicated clearly. She asked thoughtful questions. She made the entire process smooth for the brand. When she hit send, she felt nervous, hoping they would like it. When the brand responded, they didn't just like it—they adored it. They said her content captured their identity in a way no creator had done before. They posted the video, and it performed better than expected. Their comments filled with people asking about the product, loving the vibe, and appreciating Marina's authenticity. For the first time, a brand didn't move on. They came back.

A week later, the brand reached out again. They wanted to hire her for a second video. Marina felt stunned. She had never received repeat work before. She completed the second video with the same level of intention, and it performed just as well. The following month, the brand reached out a third time. They wanted consistent monthly content. They offered her a three-month contract. Marina was speechless. A long-term partnership wasn't something she believed she could achieve—yet it was happening because she had finally understood the power of exceeding expectations and building relationships.

As the months passed, the partnership deepened. The brand invited her to brainstorm ideas, sent her early access products, and included her in upcoming campaign planning. Marina wasn't just a creator to them—she had become part of their creative team. The partnership gave her financial stability, consistent income, and a stronger sense of identity. One day, the brand's founder told her something that changed her perspective forever. He said they initially hired her for the content but kept hiring her because of her professionalism, her communication, and her alignment with their brand. He said that creators like Marina were rare—creators who not only delivered quality work but also made the collaboration feel effortless.

Hearing that confirmed what she had always wondered: long-term partnerships weren't about follower count. They were about excellence, consistency, and meaningful connection. Marina had transformed from a creator chasing one-off deals into a sought-after collaborator. That skincare brand became her foundation, and through that partnership, more brands discovered her. They saw her repeated work and trusted her reliability. She built her reputation not through volume but through depth. And she finally understood a truth that changed her forever: one-off deals might pay the bills, but long-term partnerships build a career.

Epilogue

The creator economy is expanding faster than any previous digital industry, and every day more brands rely on creators to shape their marketing, influence consumer behavior, and bring authenticity to their message. While many aspiring influencers wait passively for opportunities, the creators who succeed the most understand a deeper truth: brand deals are not random; they are built through intention, identity, professionalism, and the mastery of high-impact content. Every chapter in this book has shown you that the power to create these opportunities is already in your hands. You do not need a massive following, elite connections, or expensive equipment to build a thriving sponsorship and UGC career. What you need is clarity, strategy, and consistent excellence. This epilogue is your reminder that you are not just a content creator—you are a business, a storyteller, and a partner to the brands you choose to work with.

As you step into the next phase of your creator journey, remember that your identity is the foundation of everything you will build. Brands choose creators who know who they are, what they represent, and how they communicate. Your voice, your aesthetic, your tone, and your message form the emotional signature that brands are looking for. When you stay true to your identity while refining your craft, you become recognizable. Your content becomes consistent. Your brand becomes inevitable. Every piece of content you create reinforces that identity and signals to brands that you are someone worth investing in. Never underestimate the power of clarity—because clarity is what transforms a hobby creator into a long-term partner for major companies.

Your professional presence is just as important as your artistry. The media kit you send, the pitch you write, the email you answer quickly, the contract you negotiate respectfully, and the deadlines you honor all communicate your seriousness. The creator economy is filled with talented individuals, but far fewer creators combine talent with professionalism. When you do, you become rare. And in business, rarity commands premium value. Brands do not simply want creators who can film beautiful videos; they want creators who can communicate, collaborate, and deliver. Your reliability becomes your leverage. Your consistency becomes your currency. The more dependable you are, the more doors will open—and the more long-term partnerships will follow.

Your content is your proof of value. Every beautifully lit shot, every thoughtful transition, every intentional voiceover, every emotional story you tell is a record of your growth and skill. High-impact content does not happen by accident; it is built through repetition, experimentation, and creative instinct.

When you show brands what you can do before they hire you, you speak the language of opportunity. You make it easy for them to say yes. Your content becomes a living résumé, demonstrating your ability to deliver for brands long before they ever approach you. This body of work compounds in value over time. It attracts better brands, higher budgets, and longer contracts. And with every new collaboration, your portfolio becomes stronger.

The relationships you build along the way will shape your income, your opportunities, and your stability. Brands remember creators who make their lives easier. They remember creators who show initiative, who offer ideas, who communicate clearly, and who deliver beautifully. Long-term partnerships are not based on luck—they are the result of consistent excellence and genuine connection. When a brand trusts you, they invest in you repeatedly. They expand your role. They increase your budget. They invite you into new campaigns. They refer you to other companies. One strong relationship can become the catalyst for a career transformation. Never treat a one-off collaboration as a small moment. Treat every project as a stepping stone to something bigger.

Most importantly, your mindset will determine your success. You must believe you deserve to be paid well. You must believe your creativity is valuable. You must believe your voice has impact. Too many creators limit themselves by assuming they are not worthy of sponsorships. But your uniqueness is your selling point. Your authenticity is your advantage. Your experiences, perspective, and presence cannot be replicated by anyone else—and brands are always searching for creators who bring something real, something human, something original. When you embrace your value, your confidence grows. And when your confidence grows, your career expands.

This journey is not linear. Some months will flow with opportunity; others might feel quiet. But if you remain consistent—refining your skills, optimizing your profile, nurturing brand relationships, and producing high-quality content—you will build momentum that becomes unstoppable. Sponsorships and UGC deals are not a fantasy reserved for a chosen few. They are a legitimate, profitable path available to anyone willing to master the craft and respect the business. You now have the tools, the knowledge, and the strategy to do exactly that. The creator economy rewards action, not hesitation. So move forward with intention. Build your brand with clarity. Approach opportunities with confidence. And deliver every piece of content like it has the power to change everything—because it does.

Your next collaboration is not just a deal. It is an investment in the future version of you. A version of you who is respected, well-paid, and in demand. A version of you who earns recurring income from long-term partnerships. A version of you who creates with passion and profits with purpose. That creator is already inside you. Now it's time to step fully into that identity and build the career you know you were meant to have.

www.ingramcontent.com/pod-product-compliance
Lightning Source LLC
LaVergne TN
LVHW022014200926
848481LV00007B/2378
* 9 7 9 8 2 9 5 4 6 0 4 7 0 *